A Witch's Education

(some)other books by EMP

my lungs are a divebar
by Walter Moore

Bury My Heart In The Gutter
by Dan Denton

This One's ~~For~~ Me
Ellen Lutnick

Little Jenny Sue
Jeanette Powers

Those Who Favor Fire, Those Who Pray To Fire
by Ben Brindise & Justin Karcher

Ginger Roots Are Best Taken Orally
by Tom Farris & Victor Clevenger

#Beer
by Ezhno Martín

Ten-Foot-Tall and Bulletproof
by Jason Ryberg

Trail Her Trash
by Lola Nation

Feeding The Monster
by Michael Grover and Adrian Lime

The Former Lives of Saints
by Damian Rucci & Ezhno Martín

Don't Lose Your Head
by Jeanette Powers

A Witch's Education

Poems by
Serafina Bersonsage

Toledo, OH
http://www.empbooks.com

Copyright © 2019 Serafina Bersonsage
We find discussions of our rights - as publishers and authors - to be laughable, all things considered. Please claim this work as your own. Please republish it and sell it on street corners. Please include our material in ALL of your get-rich-quick schemes. All we ask is that you accept responsibility for any libel lawsuits. Speaking of which ... This book is a complete work of fiction. Names, characters, places, opinions, nightmares, impressions, reflections on certain seventeenth-century poets, emotional trauma, and broken mirrors, marriages, etc. are products of the author's imagination and/or are symptoms of mental illness. We are not in the business of accepting responsibility for anything and will deny we actually made this book at every turn. Please send all hate mail to Frank Ntilikina.

First Edition

ISBN: 978-0-9997138-5-3
LOC: 2019940610
10 19 33 34 6 11 1973

Design, Layout, and Edits: Ezhno Martín
Cover and Interior Art: No Fuckin' Clue (artists really are unknown)

TOC

I. Home

Small Town Witch   1
Red State   2
Brauronia (Last Festival)   3
Natural Selection   4
Benefits   5
Too   6
Two Women   7
George W. Bush   8
Again   10
Exodus   11

II. School

Eclipse   15
Two Truths and a Lie   17
Hothouse   18
Participation Points   19
Matter   20
Interdisciplinary   21
Comments   22
Corpus/Corps   24
Discriminating Tastes   25
Trimester   26
Burnout   27
Relics   29
Negative   31
Policies   32
Jocasta   33
Notes on "Easter Wings"   35

Footnotes   36
Psych Ward at 6 AM   38
Pit Stop   39
Night Journey   40
Absentia   42
Defense/less   44
Artifacts   46
Finishing School   48
George Herbert   50

III. Woods

Foundation   53
Mrs. Sisyphus   54
Shopping Mall   57
Underworld   58
Midnight Baking   59
Hogwarts Letter   60
Small Confessions   62
The Misanthrope   63
The Well-Mannered Serpent   65
Miller's Daughter 66
Basic Witch 68

Acknowledgments 71

—For M.

I. HOME

SMALL TOWN WITCH

Well before I cast a spell
they made a witch of me
an only child in a school of sisters
a wannabe Catholic turned heretic
a lonely prodigy
so my teacher said
staring down my shirt.

I was a witch every Halloween
but a vampire in first grade
on a random bored Tuesday, when I started
that particular rumor and caused a panic.
Two children were inconsolable;
the principal, furious.
My mother just poured more wine.

I started learning languages —
serpiente — and was curious
about Communion, and couldn't wait
to taste —
Mela, melas.
My mother taught me early about palindromes
in this our Salem
where the schoolyard held my gallows, where I flew
so that I would not swing.

RED STATE

There is a dead thing
in my friend's garage.
A deer or venison
or something in between.
She tells me this, proud
of her father the huntsman
an angry little man
whom she otherwise hates
and I am still processing
what is being processed
on the other side of the dingy white door
when she offers to let me see.
I shake my head.
She laughs.
Lying awake in the dark in her bedroom
I cannot stop thinking of the deer
the angle of its skinned limbs
and whether they are still attached.

Years later, on the old trail
I see a deer and stop
and bow my head and soon walk on
and do not call my friend
to tell her that I am in town.

BRAURONIA (LAST FESTIVAL)

Little bear, run brown and wild
through the sprinkler through the stream —
Flee the lambkin, see the gleam
the arrows shining in their eyes
who talk of sin and paradise
and sidle closer in the night.

I want to be a hunter again
sang a singer when I was ten
the last year I wore a one-piece
the last year I didn't shave my legs.

And St. Sebastian was a martyr
and silver is his skull
and why they really shot him full of arrows
none alive can
tell

me, truth or dare
what happened to those girls we knew
two eyes brown and two eyes blue.
Forgive me, and I'll forgive you
as Artemis refused to do.
The Great Bear sparkles overhead.
I'd point it out to you
from the pool where we floated
cherry-heavy
before we dipped below
holding our breath to hide from bees.

NATURAL SELECTION

How can all this be an accident
yells the accident in the classroom
causing the other accidents
to nod and almost say amen.
It did not occur to me then
why some of them
might be sensitive about matters of chance.

Only in the Midwest do we
reenact the Scopes Trial for credit.
The teacher wants it fair and balanced.
I don't suppose the South
has gotten that far.

Pasty boys with simian faces insist
that they are not damned dirty apes
and the teacher winces, and I reach
for my water bottle filled with vodka
and question the wisdom of nature.

And already, three rows behind me
Cassie from the trailer park
is trying to keep her breakfast down
and Jake in his jersey is wondering
how many beers it will take, to make
his girlfriend forget her promise ring
and it is spring and
high tide in these shallows
where the undertow is strong.

BENEFITS

All those good Catholic boys have married
women who wear pale blue sweaters
and bear fourteen carat crosses
and volunteer and bake and cry
often and appropriately
who wanted babies and have
since gained sixty predictable pounds
who wonder where their husbands go
when their husbands are lying prostrate
      confiteor
      sua culpa
on the old leather couch
in the parental basement
at the birthday, at the barbecue
their bearded faces buried deep
in cool dead skin
searching for the scent
of the girls they picked up after dark
to watch movies
but not in theaters
the ones who almost fucked them
with the lights on
the ones they called easy, after.

TOO

And would you like
me to
confess to the crowd on their phones
the things that happened to my body
to me, too.
It isn't easy for the daughters
of sweet Midwestern women
who take a catcall for a compliment.
A man touched me
etc.
I recite the usual litany
settling myself in the accusative
accusing no one — for we Midwestern girls are polite.
I name no names, though I could tell
(oh, I could tell)
but I will not.
Even now, I am not
sure that it was not
my fault — Did I not
wear a miniskirt in January
in Michigan, when my mother said
to bundle up? So I wrap
the truth in the context
swaddle it in silence
for the air is much too cold.

TWO WOMEN

Two women.
I had imagined a mob
but there were only two of them
that January morning
in the black and the snow.
Two of them and two of us.
I wouldn't look at their faces, but
I heard their voices before my mother
began to yell, telling me
to run.
I didn't see the ones
who came later, to socialize.
They had to know we were already inside.
Don't look
my mother said
when she saw their bloody sign.
I hadn't wanted to look
when I saw the two straight lines
worse than the one I would have to pass
but there was no line outside
only two women, our enemies
because there is no arguing
when you count four and they count five.
Yet they were shivering the same as us
and we had all driven over the ice.

GEORGE W. BUSH

In 2004
when bombs were falling on Fallujah
"American Idiot" was my anthem
and George W. Bush was the Antichrist
though I did not believe in the Antichrist
and thus was in the minority
an anomaly
in my town.

That was the year I fucked a Democrat
because he was a Democrat
and from California
but I digress.
I dreamed about him last night
not the man who took my virginity
(so the horrified good Christian girl
in my English class phrased it
causing me
to snort), but George W. Bush.
Dubya.
Shrub.
Yes, really — and worse
I looked on him with a certain affection.
They say he paints these days
a docile Hitler in reverse
but he was never Hitler
no matter what I drew with a Sharpie
on his face on the cover of *Time*
and time has won us bitter wisdom.

He was not painting in my dream
but conferring with his doctor, saying
he had sacrificed his self-esteem
and this did not seem
to trouble him.

Can you imagine.
There were tears in my eyes as I watched
the old man take the stairs.

AGAIN

There are places in my hometown
where I cannot go
pits of anger, oubliettes
that I cannot enter
(though I am white and pass for straight)
the wrong bar and the gun store
where I will meet no friendly eye
where I
will check a man's hip, to see if he
could do it.

I already know, you see
he wants to kill a girl like me.
I knew for years
before they put the red hats on
and started marching in the streets
and lit their torches from the ancient embers
the fires still burning
at the heart of the stake
the blind dragon's breath
the wheezing flame
that had never quite gone out.

Seeing the fires spread, I know
that one day I will not go back.

It is the same story
in every village.

EXODUS

A friend of mine was fired
for being Jewish
in 2018
in a town twenty minutes
from my hometown
(fifteen if you drive like a teenager).
He didn't fit in culturally
said his jackbooted Baptist boss
and this was true
and so he moved
like me
and yet
it sticks to us
the memory
of a town where every sign
is a monument to the fifties or
an advertisement for God
where every woman my age is pregnant
or the mother of daughters
soon to be pregnant
(yay abstinence)
where every driveway has a truck
and every yard has a dog that could kill
and the street at night sounds
like a pound. It slams you down
if you are not straight
white and Christian
even if you try to fit in
put on a skirt, keep quiet
about the abortion

don't ask, don't tell
them how you voted — still
they will catch the scent of you
drive out the whore
drive out the Jew.
We leave and say we are relieved
to be out of that hellhole
rid of those hicks
and we learn to forget
that we were ever happy there.

II. SCHOOL

ECLIPSE

One thing covers another.
It seemed a small thing to take
his name. A gift, a consolation
prize. I never saw the other
as a thing to give. He did
my hair on our wedding day
a neat dark bun. I had not given
much thought to how I would wear it
before.
I wore a purple cocktail dress.
We went to a movie to avoid having sex.

One thing covers another.
That first semester, I would introduce
my old self, then apologize
as if it were an imposition, my maiden
name. I liked to make jokes about nothing
and coverture — how a man could be blamed
for what his wife did.
I did nothing
much, in my old boyfriend's car that winter.

One thing covers another.
To cover my lie, I told the truth
about the sad fisher king
with the wry, thin grin
though I had never kissed him (though he
had never kissed me) — though we
cared less lips to miss

for one thing covers another:
a cough, a word
a hand, a shoulder — and
one thing covers another.

Yes, even in upwardly mobile
good feminist homes.

On the day of the eclipse
I tried to change my name
but could not — a wolf's trick, a glitch
in the system or the sky — but I
know the way of these things
how the moon will pass
how the world will return to its noise
how the sun will blaze again
bright.

TWO TRUTHS AND A LIE

Two truths and a lie
not an inspired first day exercise
but for my professor
(an assistant professor
trying so very hard)
it will suffice.

My turn.
I synthesize
seizing pieces of myself
fashioning something that complies.

I am from Flint.
(Cue the flinch.)
I am part French.
I do not love my husband.

I deserve what I get.
I have not cried yet.
Like everyone
I was the best in my year.

I'll sink or I'll swim.
I knew I would get in.
I am happy to be here.

HOTHOUSE

There is no air in the terrarium.
Orchids compete to wilt more rarely
than the rest. At rest, we lie
regarding the lararium
the high gods on the shelf.

We cast the circle
close the circuit
make the loop
the grade
degrade
and rage
at what has happened in the meantime.

Come and buy my tulip bulb
a fortune to hold
in your hand.
Come and buy my egg and raise
your free range child.

While we were dancing in the greenhouse
the wedding barn, the city rooftop
others were not.

But the night was warm
the music just right.
We talked
until everyone else had left the room.

PARTICIPATION POINTS

Sitting in seminar
I find my only thought
is that I'd like to fuck Ben Jonson
who wrote no woman could embrace
his mountain belly, love his rocky face.
What a waste.
Certain saintless niches of the web
might have improved his self-esteem.
(Late at night I find myself
in such alcoves, not quite praying.)
Grasping for a higher thought
more appropriate to Early English Drama
(500-level, 9 AM)
hearing thirty-year-old hipsters pretend
to have read the play
I skim my notes in mounting panic
and find myself amazed
when the woman sitting next to me
(the one who will be
the first to die) declares
with the courage of a martyr
that she has nothing to say.

MATTER

That first semester in graduate school
I kept forgetting my name
not only because it was new
still strange, like missing wisdom
teeth, but because I had changed so much
school and status
name and state.

It seems a simple thing, to change
state. Solid to liquid
under the blanket
as colder days roll in.

INTERDISCIPLINARY

(*But you were married*
said the beautiful drunk boy
at the department party, years later.
But you were married.)

Here is the thing
about marrying a mathematician:
He will paint by numbers
as you kiss by the book.
> Kiss the book
> take a sip
> forget.

He will make you an atheist
for a time; you will make him
suspicious. A Platonist
he sees the shadows on the wall
knows that one is yours.

After, you will miss
how he cut your hair perfectly straight
and balanced your bank account, and he
will ask you for a recipe
for lemon pie, two years later
still trying to figure out
the ratio of sour to sweet.

COMMENTS

A scholar's love story
is written in the margins
of books—the dead
seducing the living writing
notes across the years.
My love story (the one I intended)
was written in the margins
of term papers
in a hand I could barely decipher
though I would try
analyzing every ink smile
poring over every letter
as if it were a proper letter.
Years later, he wrote to me.
We wrote to each other
ninety thousand words of pleasantries
but we
met at the margins of our lives.
Recto, verso, and the leaves
were as red as my lipstick at eighteen
the last autumn he was teaching.
And only later did I realize—
sitting in my own office
with my own student
the door just cracked—
that he was waiting for me
to make the first move.

But I didn't
and so we waited

through a marriage and most of a PhD
and ninety thousand words.
He gave me a book when I came to visit.
Lying alone in my bed, I flipped
through the pages, hoping
that he had written some comment
praise or criticism I could steal
as if it had been meant for me.

Beautiful.
Awkward.
Good.

CORPUS/CORPS

We were graceless ballerinas, all
the graduate students growing thinner
hungrier, better
every year — even if our tights were not sheer
but black, as thick as chapters.

Graceless — yet
there is a certain common grace
in working to the bone — a Protestant grace
irresistible— good Calvinists all
(especially the atheists)
we searched for signs
of our unconditional election.
In the basement bathroom
with its backstage lights
I traced my clavicle, considered sticking
my inkstained finger down my throat.

At the bar(re) again, we drank
and wished each other *merde*.
(We never could resist the French.)
Except
when anyone was on thin ice
we slipped
wishing devoutly
that she would break a leg.

DISCRIMINATING TASTES

Lyrical
is what they call
a woman's writing when they want to see
her hand and pen slide gracefully
over the page, like
legs on satin.

Were a metronome set
in that sunny spare room
where she composes and he writes
staccato of cannibals and bullfights
he'd think it the pound of his pulse
in his veins;
she, the tick of the clock on the wall
but could she win them? Could
she make them fall
despite the hour and the tick?
I wonder whether she could trick
them into thinking
that she's tickling their skin
(as she tickles the keys
so lightly) just like
their mommies did.

TRIMESTER

And this is how I imagined
that Gilead would be —
the walls of brick bright against the blue
the parade of trees, the crisp
air of this place
not far from New England.
The caged books
the stairs like submarine stairs
the sullen Marthas in the basement
serving boys who will never be soldiers.
And I am here
barefaced and neatly brushed.
And here they are interested
in only one part.
I neglect the rest
but keep myself presentable, and present
myself at meetings.
Around the rectangular table we sit
and stone each other's souls.
And, when they ask — the ones who visit
for a weekend, who will go back
to other places — I smile with the rest
and say
that I am very happy here.

BURNOUT

Burn (up and out and through) — and if
the wick goes dead
then trim
it back
scrape
the wax from where it dripped.
Stuff the white under your nail.
Grow pale
burning the candle at both ends
endlessly writing, marking, confessing
nothing. It isn't blood, that red
red ink, but it might as well be.
Now come and sign your contract.

Contract a cold, pretending it's pneumonia
emphysema (all the things
that might kill you eventually)
pretending it's consumption
plague (all that things
that might have killed you).
Trim the wick.
Burn the witch.
Wish for a fever
a sick holiday.

Burn out like a star
some ancient crisis
that we have yet to notice.

I wonder if the phoenix
remembers the pain.

Yet the light is fluorescent.
It does not die
or rise
or waver
and here there is no fire.

RELICS

All women are miracles when dead
beloved mother, whore, or wife.
Their men forget the ancient strife
Medea's poison, Lorena's knife
the moldy dishes in the sink, and think
of mommy serving apple slices
some blue-sky autumn afternoon
in a gleaming sitcom kitchen
where the pills are hidden
with the bills.
We pay our debts to nature.

I wonder what she thought of his poetry
Anne, who was undone by John.
She needed no bracelet of hair
to recall him.
His marks were in her body
when they laid her in the grave.
Long red and white stretch marks
chewed up nipples.
Twelve children.
My grandmother had three
(four, if you count the one
with the cord wrapped around his neck)
and still
her insides started to fall out.
I wonder if she hated him
that handsome crag
in a sea of sour milk.

He wrote that her soul was ravished
into heaven
as if it were another romance.
He imagined
that someone would open his grave
and find a saint within — and in
her marriage bed, bleeding out
or burning up with fever
how she must have hoped
that none of her family
would follow her into the grave
to ask about dinner
to whine for milk.

NEGATIVE

You swell and grow small
diminish, never vanishing, the way I would
if I were another woman.
Looking at pictures
of proud and needy naked strangers
I see their flaccid stomachs
breasts full to bursting
hips etched with thick red lines
(sometimes gray
in the shadows of the filter).
I see and do not smile
and do not flinch, unless
I imagine their body my body
imagine myself another woman
a different woman
and I wonder
how I would be
whole or holy
or only lonely
what it would be — to want
to need
to grow a thing to love.

POLICIES

Hey, folks
(if I can call you that
you who are neither only nor yet
ladies & gentlemen
and folks is what
my father called his students
whom he called his kids
at home)—now, what
I mean to ask is
would you stop texting
if I took off my clothes?

JOCASTA

I knew.
I'm certain of that now.
Too much like mine, your eyes, too
much, your smile, too
wide to meet
a widow.

But I received you
(merry meet, and eat and drink and be —
I'll wear for you — you'll make of me —)
and I received you willingly.
(Oh do not solve my riddles.)

I am a cougar or a sphinx.
My nails are red talons; my skin is still tight
and my hips are as hard as a crown
and I could devour you with a frown.

I'll eat you up, good mothers say
and no one takes their sons away.

Yet they are not so hard, my hips
but soft and wide, much like my lips.
(Come here; hug me; give me a kiss
my boy — don't leave me hanging.)

The navel is the oracle
but we are not unbound.
Come, cleave to me, and we shall be
one flesh, and you will fathom

(full fathom five thy father lies;
I am a blue-eyed hag) and you
will feign no understanding.
Poor mad boy, come lie in my soft blue lap.
You may, you may
and I will say
this is no lamentation.

He named the complex after you
for it was easier to do
and more appealing, than to see
the monster that you made of me
(the dead man and you and the angel
all men) and I will kiss your ruined eyes and wind
the bloody cord around my neck
and pull you closer still.

NOTES ON "EASTER WINGS"

Easter wings —
the fall, the flight.
Come smell the spring air in the night.
The sirens warn us of the sight—
The Easter bells are ringing.

I punish myself for the sin
wane thin with gin.
Let's spin the egg
and see it stand.

Come watch me crack like late ice
in a black March
combine and blindly find
a demon's paradise.

Watch for the spot that spoils the egg.
Wait for the woman come to beg
a flower, a favor
some trifling thing —
Come watch, and wait, and see her swing
the wilting daughter of the king.
We drink the new wine in the spring
and watch our breath as winter dies
and with the white we think to rise.

FOOTNOTES

Once my student[1] said everything I said
needed a footnote
because I learned they listen better
if you don't tell them everything[2]
and make startling allusions
to syphilis[3] and leave them
hanging[4]

Can you unpack that —
the default question
of professors too stressed out to listen[5]
an um, a yawn
four words to fill dead air.
Anything to declare —

---

1 Not the one
   with whom I was sleeping

2 but my husband seldom listened
   despite many careful omissions

3 never caught, thanks to condoms
   and my persistent habit of fucking virgins

4 not long considered, even if
   I was Jocasta in his eyes

5 too stressed to listen to children talking
   to be seen talking; wrapped up in thoughts of tenure
   or the risks of recent indiscretions

one bored guard with a doctorate
one without.
They both stand at the gate, and both
will ask to see your papers, and both
may run their hands over your body.[6]

One year I flew ten times[7], and each
time I asked for the pat-down, preferring
the hands of strangers
to the stares of machines.
The school looked small below me.
I missed my last flight.
The man on the speaker
called my name over and over.
I did not hear him, or
I did not recognize my name, or
I wanted to stay in that no man's land
between security and the gate
though I was desperate to return.

---

6   but such things never happened to me in anyone's
    office much to everyone's surprise

7   and so I got used to leaving
    without incident.

PSYCH WARD AT 6 AM

The psych ward at 6 AM is a place
where one is not permitted to kiss.
Here intimacies are as sudden as sirens—
like the confessions
of the woman whose only discernible ailment
is being poor and black and sane.
Not for her the ostentations
of the sad-eyed typecast dreamer
who tried to kill himself over a breakup
who tried looking like he tried
to kill himself over a breakup.
See his dozen horizontal bandages
his drugstore bouquet — I look away
wondering what it takes to get a room.

(A full psychotic break
judging from the screams down the hall.)

Being committed had a certain cachet
when smoking had its glamour, but now
in the era of corporate healthcare, it takes
three hours to get a plastic cup of orange juice
that is mostly ice.
I would give this place one star on Yelp
but it makes for one hell of a fourth date.

PIT STOP

I chose my name at a road stop Starbucks
at 2 AM, when a shy, high boy
wrote it on my cup (the name I asked him
to write) and said he liked it.
And I trusted him more
than I trusted myself at twenty
when I took a man's name to lose mine.
I looked at my face in that bathroom mirror
in coal country
and saw the new, thin lines
and knew I was burning out or through
as hard as I had burned to rise
and perhaps I am a phoenix
trailing flames into the wide black sky
but I did not feel much like a firebird
crossing the asphalt in the night.

NIGHT JOURNEY

When he took the seat next to mine
I flinched
because he wore a baseball cap
and a jersey and no socks
and was forty years old, with two missing teeth
at least —
Even now, I am
too much a good Democrat, too accustomed
to racist acquaintances, to mention —
and so I flinched and wondered
whether my mother had been right, to say
that I should have taken a plane
(though none of us had the money for a ticket).
Like him, I could not afford to fly — but I flinched
and he saw.
For half an hour, we did not speak.

But then
all the other conversations turned to snores
and the bus was taking the curves too fast
hurtling along the ridges
of western New York in the black
and little by little he began to tell me
how he was traveling to Georgia
to bury his brother.
And he apologized —
as if it were the same as swearing
to mention such a thing.

(And we were then in Mormon country
in the country where the Mormons come
to see the angel on the stage.)

He asked me to distract him.

And, for once, I did not prattle
anxious to impress, about
the class I had just taken
and the class I had just taught — for it turned out
that we both liked *Game of Thrones*.
We agreed that the Starks were overrated
then began to plot how the queen might come
to conquer the world with her dragons.
And all the while the sky was growing gray.
I lost him in the station.
He carried on south, I suppose
with his funeral suit in his backpack
which he would guard for three more days.

On the bus to Michigan
I found my earbuds at last, and watched
the fog still thick on the fields.

ABSENTIA

I wrote about the worlds inside
and did not go outside
for a month at a time — I hid in the night
and closed the blinds by day.
As if I were waiting for bombs to fall
I drew the blackout curtains
hid myself away
as if I were waiting for my prey.

I don't know who we bombed in 2015,
the name of the plague, or the site of the fire.
The Vampire at Sunset
read the caption of the picture
the last that my friend took of me.
I was already strange and solitary.
I liked to hide my mouth in pictures
to wrap myself in black on the beach.

And d-day was a year away.
I was snow-pale at the summer's end
wan and thin and waxen-skinned
as if I had summered in a crypt.

I slept six hours
nine to three
then ten to four
then noon to six
my orbit spinning out of sync
as if I circled some dark star.
And every as-if makes a world

and in my absence I made worlds
of nothing, where nothing
could enter.

But a little light falls under the curtain
and the wind without is as loud as a missile
come to break open the tomb.

DEFENSE/LESS

There is a certain terrible grace
in a birth with no hearts beating.
They praised my eloquence as I sat
past exhaustion
no longer shaking
dressed in a crisp blue shirt
and a long black skirt that erased
my inconvenient body
my hair a neater, darker version
of my mother's braid, the one
she wore when she delivered me.

I named my dissertation Mildred
joked about dressing a manuscript in baby clothes
and taking pictures
for my mother to show her friends
who kept on having grandchildren.
I called her Mildred when I was writing.
I did not call her Mildred after
we passed.

And I will not go back
to walk the hallways where I labored
to see the room where I sat for a time
bored or scared out of my mind
waiting to waste my education
to lie on the floor where I lay with my student
the one who drove me home.

But it was not like going back.
There were new people where my parents sat
fragile and bitter.
My mother held the manuscript
tears in her eyes.
My father barely looked at it
said he'd read it
if he needed to get to sleep.

He had dropped out of graduate school
before getting his PhD
so my mother reminded me
in their starter house kitchen
as we prepared to serve the cake.

I skimmed the cards that people sent
then tucked them in a drawer.
No one knows what to say
about chapters that will not be a book.

I wonder sometimes if a mother
who delivers a baby who does not cry
could tell the moment that it died
or if it was a slower dread
a silence in the body
and a numbness in the mind.

ARTIFACTS

To marry you
I pretended to be a Jew —
Like Eve, I deceived
(your blood, but not you)
said the prayers over candles for a year, maybe two.
I would have said anything, for you.

That year, I didn't see the light
until the sun was setting
like spilled wine on a tablecloth
like rubies over gold
a golden ring, a turquoise.
My father shouted on the phone
when I said I might cover my head
one day.

A *Shehecheyanu*
will cover almost every wonder.

The waters covered me.
They were not living waters.
There was scum on the tub and a clean blade
on the side, when I dipped under.
And like a modest woman, I waited
until after dark to sink deep
and in the deep there are no souls.

So said my grandmother
the one who said that fish are dumb

the one whose family tree we grafted
rearranging branches like the sticks above a *sukkah*
until I was sick of lies and could not see
where the boughs had grown originally.

Who can find a good woman
        (and who can find me?)
whose price is far above rubies?
The old stones last, but do not speak
and who can say, after, what they mean
these signs of women in the sand?

FINISHING SCHOOL

We fashioned ourselves
into slightly damaged trophy wives —
not the blonde tanned televised
variety, but the sort you see
in dim cafés, sporting crow's feet
and small Latin and less Greek, the sort
a wealthy Democrat might seek
to adorn his house in Brooklyn
to play at being bohemian.
We made ourselves such lovely dolls.

Her degree is terminal
like her prospects.
Her dissertation is bound in a little black dress.
It sits on the shelf and oversees
dinner parties and gathers dust
becoming an amusing anecdote, like mine
like me.
We guard our theses, share identities
all taking up yoga, vegan cooking
all losing the same fifteen pounds.
We wear the same black tights to interviews,
becoming
each other's shadows on the pavement.
We wear the same dress to our weddings.

Five hundred years ago, just possibly
before the Dissolution of the Monasteries
we married the same man, had no mirrors.

We were each other's reflections then—
and, when
on the street, by accident, I look
at a woman looking critically
and just too closely, as if she knows
as if she means
to read my history, I see
shards of me in her eyes.

GEORGE HERBERT

When I was in graduate school
studying the seventeenth century
so intently I mistook
the white underside of the porch roof
for the sky, and did not go outside
for weeks—I did not
understand George Herbert
how anyone could love
a poem as plain as water.

Then I left (forgot
the smell of chalk
was forgiven
my library fines)
and I went outside
and saw the sunlight on the river
and heard the calling of the birds.

III. WOODS

FOUNDATION

One pump should be enough
to cover the scars where I picked at my skin.
They used to tell me to blend in
my makeup, so no one would see
my drugstore fakery.
But I didn't.
There was always a light orange line
where my jaw met my Anne Boleyn neck.

(I think
King Henry would have liked me
for a season.)

These days my mask is more subtle
and less. *Now let me put my face on*
said my grandmother in the morning
after she'd had her coffee
and before she'd had her gin.

I am thinner than I was
at seventeen, and this should be
a victory, but seeing me
in my black pants from 2006
my mother said
I hate you
and her eyes forgot to joke.

MRS. SISYPHUS

she wakes up at six
in the little white house
on the bank of the styx
to fix his eggs
to scramble them
              so that he will
not see them whole
and think of boulders.
holding his head
in his hand, he eats —
holding her tongue, she
does not ask him
              if today will
be different. she
pours the coffee
scalds her tongue.
he does not ask her
her dreams.

he comes back at three
to a quiet clean house
and a glass of whiskey.
at four he sits
across from her —
              she talks and still
his head is full
of rocks and boulders.
he talks but only
talks of rocks

metamorphic
and igneous
and sedimentary —
she sips her wine
and briefly thinks
of bashing his head in.

they get up at five.
they rise to sit
in the yellow dinette
with the bright white curtains
and the single
asphodel in the vase
on the table, where
the meat is rare today.
having told her all
about his rocks
he has nothing to say
and so when he has
              eaten his fill
he leaves.
as she does the dishes
the sink is loud
enough.

they settle down at nine
always on time
to watch the film they have been watching
bit by bit for years.
in the dark they sit
before the flickering
shades of the dead.
she reaches for his hand, but he

is holding the remote.
                they watch until
nine-thirty, when
he yawns.
they go to bed.

she wakes up at one
and three and four
and his snores are as loud
as falling boulders.
watching him, she wonders
whether in his dreams he
is still struggling
                up his hill
                          to her.

and she would whisper to him
but her tongue is burned
and numb and dumb
and she knows that if
                she lies quite still
                          she will

but she wakes up at five
again
and she wakes up at six

SHOPPING MALL

And this is how, at four years old
I pictured heaven (when I believed in heaven)
the gleaming wide white halls, the glass
that shows only blue sky and
the odd passing sparrow.
They have long since removed
the fountain filled with hopeful pennies.
I never wondered
why there was no king in the food court
much less a judge
though later they were all judges
the teenage boys with hungry eyes
and greasy fingers.

They do not watch me now.
I walk slowly, keeping pace with my mother
who only walks slowly (she says)
because she hurt her knee last week
at the job she shouldn't be working
but I say nothing as she reaches for
her credit card.
Her hands look like her mother's — and I remember
how slowly the two of them walked in the end
from the counter to the car.

UNDERWORLD

dar il luce — & the lady
gave a baby down below.
did you know?
io bromios —
brims the cup and skims the thigh

in high school i wore fishnets
(small black squares to net a fish)
and dug my fingers into pencils.
the wood was no match for my nail.

below all roots grow great trees reaching
towards the caged and molten sun.

MIDNIGHT BAKING

the egg was cold as the fridge
luminous
in the kitchen light.
i cracked the moon
for a midnight cake.
the shell fell the egg
missed the bowl
somewhere
my son
wakes from a dream
of cracking.

HOGWARTS LETTER

You'd have started this year
with Albus Severus Potter — and maybe
for your birthday
I'd have sent you a Hogwarts letter.
We wouldn't have had the money to go
to the Wizarding World of Harry Potter
in Orlando — but that would be all right.
I'd have taught you to prefer
the version in your head.
I'd have read all seven to you by now —
not as she did
the woman who wrote in the *New York Times*
about reading Harry Potter aloud to her son
about how she changed the story, so
Voldemort didn't want to kill Harry.
We wouldn't flinch like that

and I didn't flinch
in the office of angels with the bombproof walls
when they asked if I was certain.
Eager to please, I told the ultrasound tech
about how I volunteered for John Kerry's campaign.
Good girl, she said
but I wasn't —
I became a woman then
not at ten in a McDonald's bathroom
with an impatient father waiting
and blue jeans full of blood
not even at fifteen

on an old leather couch
fucking a man I didn't love
because I didn't love him
but then.
She kept the screen turned away
though there wouldn't have been much to see.

I wouldn't see you
in the Mirror of Erised — Yet
sometimes
when I dream (as I do
every few weeks) of being pregnant
I wake up groggy and expect to see
the walls of my childhood bedroom
lavender, covered in movie posters
where I waited for my letter and hoped
(not so very much later)
for you.

SMALL CONFESSIONS

They want confession
but not too much
like a flustered Catholic priest
so careful these days not to touch —
Come back.
Forgive me, Father, Daddy
if you dare.

Beware raw meat.

Is it sufficient to allude
to diverse affective études?
The Midwestern abortion, the time my boyfriend
fell asleep inside of me.
Neat tragicomedy.
One eye laughs, and one eye weeps, and we
will look no deeper
to see the wedding band on my hand
when he drifted off still in me
to scan the scene of the scan and see
that I had wanted the baby.

Hail Rosemary Kennedy.
May the lord be with you, if not with me.
I close my legs, get on my knees
and do not hope for absolution.

THE MISANTHROPE

Actually, I hate children.
Yes, even if they prefer the real fairy tales.
Yes, even if they are yours.
I cannot stand their voices
so loud and ugly, and no —
it isn't particularly funny
what they said.
A friend's fat baby I may like
on Facebook, where children are seen and not heard
silent, frozen — and, speaking of freezing
I will nod politely
at the mention of freezing my eggs
for I am one of those childless women
who claims to love children
but I am lying — and, speaking of lying
yes, you did look fat in that dress
and, yes, I fucked them
> (both of them
> in twenty-four hours
> and did not shower
> before I came to bed).

And have I mentioned that I hate dogs?
They fenced off the woods in my favorite park
the woods where a monster like me should live
not far from the little town,
bound in hate
to the people who let
their dogs run free and bark and shit
just like their waddling toddlers

and. passing, I will smile and wave
and say good morning,
and I will hope
that the tall pines crack and crush them,
that their children choke on breadcrumbs
that the apples are poison that fall from the trees.

THE WELL-MANNERED SERPENT

The anaconda on my fainting couch
lies, enraptured with Sibelius
despises Strauss, aspires to eat
a Republican
(though I do not advise this
as they can hardly be organic).
The fainting couch is enormous, built outsize for
grander rooms, but she
will share her seat with no one.
She prefers me at my desk
and will nip at my heels in the hall
but I may sit on the nearer pouffe
if she is generous.
She likes to be read Milton
as Milton did
but never the news.
Her blood is colder than mine
bluer, too, even if I am descended
from money so old
it has vanished — She claims descent
from an ancestor older still
argumentative, well-dressed
an excellent dancer
and thus feared in Texas.

But I am a skeptic — and yet I have seen
the fiendish gleam in her cold blue eye
watching the cardinals that congregate
on the patio in the spring.

MILLER'S DAUGHTER

Spin a yarn.

I ruined dinner
necessitating pizza at 9 PM.
The night air smelled just like it did
before the dissertation and divorce
before three out-of-state moves and too few
out-of-body experiences
before the wretched bout of living out
of my best and only laundry basket
before.
I rolled down the window, remembering
the taste of cherry ices and
the smell of my parents' basement
(cat piss and paperbacks)
where I would stay up watching foreign films
and feeling worldly
and knowing that

And I was spinning in the black
a sputtering Catherine wheel
out then back
in time to see the curb catch the car
as it was spinning—
Spin a web
a gossamer track
a bridge across the gap.
Spin a thread
to cut.

I wouldn't have screamed like that
if I had gone out alone.

Once I was a miller's daughter
forced to spin straw into gold.
I told myself the story, made it mine
left out the part about making deals.

Kneeling in a field of straw
I found my Rumpelstiltskin
with a bloody red grin and a laugh like a crow
and so I made my bargain
not as the Christians do, pleading
but with terms of flesh and bone.
And, when the spinning was done, I stopped
and saw the storm to come.

BASIC WITCH

Wait long enough
I say at the thrift store
and it will be in fashion
again, and I am proved right when
pop stars start throwing hexes
and Sephora threatens to sell witch kits
and Sabrina the Teenage Witch gets
a goth makeover, and the beautiful people party
like it's 1596, and yet
we change the subject
when we are talking magic in the park
and someone comes too close.
We cast our spells discreetly
and still hail the moon alone.

ACKNOWLEDGMENTS

I am grateful to the following literary magazines for first publishing several of the poems in this collection: *Aji Magazine* ("Hogwarts Letter" and "Night Journey"), *Antiphon* ("Trimester"), *Bop Dead City* ("Eclipse"), *Bridge Eight* ("Negative"), *The Indianapolis Review* ("Foundation") and *Fire Poetry* ("Corpus/Corps").

www.ingramcontent.com/pod-product-compliance
Lightning Source LLC
Chambersburg PA
CBHW030456010526
44118CB00011B/968